D0922635

FRESH AND DRIED
FLOWERS

Inspirational arrangements for beautiful floral displays

LORENZ BOOKS

This edition first published in 1999 by Lorenz Books

© Anness Publishing Limited 1999

Lorenz Books is an imprint of Anness Publishing Limited
Hermes House, 88–89 Blackfriars Road
London SE1 8HA

This edition is distributed in Canada by Raincoast Books,
8680 Cambie Street, Vancouver, British Columbia, V6P 6M9

All rights reserved. No part of this publication may be reproduced, stored in a retrieval system, or
transmitted in any way or by any means, electronic, mechanical, photocopying, recording or
otherwise, without the prior written permission of the copyright holder.

ISBN 1 85967 944 7

A CIP catalogue record for this book is available from the British Library.

Publisher: Joanna Lorenz
Project Editors: Fiona Eaton and Emma Clegg
Designer: Lilian Lindblom
Jacket Designer: Ian Sandom
Illustrators: Anna Koska, Nadine Wickenden
Contributors: Fiona Barnett, Tessa Evelegh, Lucinda Ganderton, Terence Moore, Pamela Westland
Photography: James Duncan, Michelle Garrett, Nelson Hargreaves, Debbie Patterson

Previously published as two separate titles: 30 Dried Flower Displays and 30 Fresh Flower Displays

Printed and bound in Singapore

1 3 5 7 9 10 8 6 4 2

CONTENTS

INTRODUCTION

Fresh and dried flowers offer untold possibilities for creative displays, whether they are used to decorate the home on an everyday basis or for a very special occasion such as a wedding or a Christmas party. And with the enormous improvement in the availability, quality and range of commercially grown flowers in recent years, you can enjoy beautiful displays all year round.

While in the past displays were structured by formal rules, a less rigid approach now allows the flower arranger more freedom to interpret flower arrangements in their own way, and there is a strong emphasis on natural designs. Of course, modern flower arranging still relies on the basic principles of colour, scale, proportion and balance, but it uses them in what is often a very simple way to create adventurous designs in exciting colour and textural combinations.

Similarly, improvements in the preservation of plant materials have resulted in a tremendous increase in the types of dried flower and the introduction of vibrant new colours. Contemporary dried flower displays emphasize colour and texture by using massed materials so that their collective strength defines the creative impact. Other natural elements, such as moss and twigs, fir cones and raffia, can also be integrated to great effect with dried flowers.

This book presents a wealth of ideas for floral decoration in the home and to mark special occasions. Creating inspirational displays using fresh and dried flowers, with results ranging from elegant simplicity to formal splendour, requires no special training or knowledge, simply plenty of enthusiasm, a little practice and an extra touch of imagination.

Fresh Flowers

To some, arranging fresh flowers is an all-consuming passion, but to many it remains a mystery. It is, in fact, an activity which can be enjoyed by anyone with readily available materials and no elaborate equipment or training. You just need enthusiasm to get started. Full of inspiration and practical ideas, the projects which follow also include arrangements for special occasions.

FLOWER CARE AND CONDITIONING

Whether you are picking a posy from the garden or choosing some blooms from a local florist, it is important to recognize flowers in their peak condition. Once you have purchased your flowers, there are a number of things you can do to make sure you get the best from them for as long as possible.

CHOOSING FLOWERS

Most flowers should be picked or purchased when they are in bud with several coloured petals showing. For spike-shaped flowers like eremurus (foxtail lily) or delphinium, make sure some of the florets are open. Flowers such as narcissi, and particularly daffodils, may be picked or bought in tight green buds as they open very quickly when placed in water.

Conversely, gerbera (Transvaal daisies) and chrysanthemums are both sold fully open, but they can last for at least two weeks. Check to see that no petals have brown edges and ensure that leaves are green and healthy with no traces of brown.

TIPS FOR MAXIMIZING THE LIFE SPAN OF FRESH FLOWERS

1 Ensure that flowers are not left out of water, as the stem ends dry out quickly. To transport, cover the stem ends with damp newspaper and wrap the flowers in paper or cellophane (plastic wrap) to avoid excess evaporation and wilting.

2 If you are taking flowers from the garden, pick them in the cool of the morning or evening and place them in water immediately.

3 Before arranging, all flowers appreciate a long, cool drink in deep water for as long as possible, preferably overnight.

4 Always trim the flower stem ends with a long, clean diagonal cut which gives the maximum area for taking up water. Woody stems should be cut in the same way. Never crush stems with a hammer, as this damages the cell structure.

5 Remove any lower foliage that will be submerged in the vases. Any leaves that remain underwater will start to rot quickly, and the resulting bacteria then blocks the flower stems and makes the water look and smell unpleasant.

6 Make sure that vases and containers are completely clean before use. Use fresh, tepid water, as this contains the least amount of air. If air bubbles get into the stems they can cause a blockage, restricting the flow of water and causing wilting or drooping flower heads.

7 Always add flower food to the water. It contains the right amount of sugar needed to encourage buds to open, and a mild disinfectant that inhibits the growth of the bacteria that cause flower heads to droop and foliage to wilt prematurely.

8 Keep flowers in a cool, well-ventilated atmosphere, well away from icy draughts (drafts) or hot fires in winter and direct sunlight in summer. The ethylene gas that is produced by mature fruit and vegetables is detrimental to flowers as it speeds up the ripening process.

9 Check flower vases regularly and fill them up with water in hot weather when it evaporates more quickly. However, when using flower food it is unnecessary to change the water.

10 Remove any drying flowers and leaves, as these faded blooms may affect the longevity of other flowers in the vase.

WILTING FLOWERS

There is a useful technique for strengthening flowers with soft, flexible, weak stems such as gerbera or those that have simply wilted. Take a group of flowers and wrap the top three-quarters of their stems together in paper to keep them erect, then stand them in deep, cool water for about two hours. The cells within the stems will fill with water and the flowers will be able to stand on their own once more when the paper is removed.

FOLIAGE

Generally the rules for conditioning foliage are the same as for the flowers. As well as stripping the lower leaves, cut the stem base at an angle. It is also important to scrape the bark 6 cm (2½ in) from the bottom of the stem and then split it to further encourage the absorption of water. This effectively prolongs the life of the foliage.

SPRING BLOSSOM URN

The explosion of plant life in the spring is visually depicted in this arrangement of early flowers and foliage. Heavily flowered heads of white lilac are the focal blossoms of the display set against the dark brown stems of pussy willow and cherry.

MATERIALS

urn
cellophane (plastic wrap)
1 block plastic foam
scissors
stub (floral) wires
reindeer moss
15 stems pussy willow
10 stems white lilac
15 stems pink cherry blossom

1 Line the urn with cellophane (plastic wrap) and wedge in the water-soaked block of plastic foam. Trim away the excess cellophane.

2 Make hairpins from stub (floral) wires and pin reindeer moss into the plastic foam around the urn rim.

3 Arrange the pussy willow in the urn to establish the height and width of a symmetrical outline.

4 Distribute the lilac throughout the pussy willow.

5 Position the pink cherry blossom throughout the display in order to reinforce the overall shape.

TULIP ARRANGEMENT

Sometimes the simple beauty of an arrangement that relies entirely on one type of flower in its own foliage can be breathtaking. This display of 'Angelique' tulips in glorious profusion contains nothing to compete with their soft pastel pink colour and would make a dramatic room centrepiece.

MATERIALS

*50 stems 'Angelique' tulips
watertight container
such as a small bucket
basket
scissors*

1 Strip the lower leaves from the tulips to prevent them from rotting in the water. Fill the bucket with water and place in the basket.

2 Cut each tulip stem to the correct size and place the stems in the water. Start building the display from its outside edge inwards.

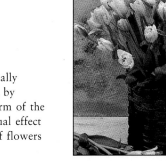

TIP

The arrangement is technically relatively unstructured but, by repetition of the regular form of the tulip heads, the overall visual effect is that of a formal dome of flowers to be viewed in the round.

3 Continue arranging the tulips towards the centre of the display until a full and even domed shape is achieved. You should be able to view the display from all sides.

THE MODERN APPROACH

*A tall, wide cylindrical vase, spatter-painted to harmonize with the wall
behind it, is on just the right lines for a low-key floral display in a modern setting.*

MATERIALS

*plastic-coated wire
mesh netting
tall, wide cylindrical vase
scissors
florist's adhesive tape
3 stems acanthus leaves
10 stems Lilium longiflorum
5 stems white roses
5 stems cream roses
2 stems eucalyptus
8 stems pampas grass*

1 Crumple the wire mesh netting into a ball and fit it into the neck of the container. Cut and thread two lengths of adhesive tape through the netting, criss-cross them over the container and stick the ends close to the rim, where they will be concealed by the lowest of the plant materials. Arrange the acanthus stems so that the leaves form a bowl shape to outline the flowers, with the tallest stems at the back and the shortest ones at the front.

2 Position the lily stems so that the fully opened flowers are pointing in different directions – some forward, some to the right, and some to the left. In this way you can appreciate the full beauty of these flowers in silhouette.

3 Cut off all but the topmost rose leaves. Split the ends of the rose stems to facilitate water intake.

4 Arrange the roses so that they nestle among the lily stems and give an overall roundness to the design. Add eucalyptus sprays to trail over the container rim, and a few strands of pampas grass at one side.

SPRING NAPKIN DECORATION

*The sophisticated gold and white colour combination used in these
elegant and delicate napkin decorations would be perfect for a formal dinner.*

MATERIALS

small-leaved ivy trails (sprigs)
napkins
scissors
1 pot lily-of-the-valley
1 pot tiny cyclamen
(*dwarf* Cyclamen persicum)
gold cord

1 Wrap an ivy trail (sprig) around the middle of a rolled napkin. Tie the stem in a knot. Using 4–5 stems of lily-of-the-valley and 3 cyclamen flowers on their stems, create a small flat-backed sheaf by spiralling the stems.

2 Place one cyclamen leaf at the back of the lily-of-the-valley for support and place two more around the cyclamen flowers to emphasize the focal point. Tie at the binding point with gold cord. Lay the sheaf on top of the napkin and ivy, wrap gold cord around the napkin and stems, gently tying it into a bow.

TIED POSY

Flowers are at their most appealing when kept simple. Just gather together some garden cuttings and arrange them in a pretty posy that the recipient can simply unwrap and put straight into a vase, without further ado.

MATERIALS

secateurs (pruning shears)
5 stems pink roses
10 stems eucalyptus
8 stems scabious
brown paper
ribbon

1 Using secateurs (pruning shears), cut each flower stem to approximately 15 cm (6 in) long. Gather the flowers together, surrounding each rose with some feathery eucalyptus, and then add the scabious.

2 Wrap the posy with paper and tie it with a pretty ribbon bow.

GEOMETRY LESSON

*Whoever would have thought, when learning about right-angled triangles,
that the knowledge would be put to use in a flower arrangement!
This design, an interpretation of the classic "L-shape", is composed on a
stoneware dish which has, by contrast, gentle curves.*

MATERIALS

scissors
florist's adhesive clay
pinholder
shallow waterproof dish such as
a baking or serving dish
10 stems slender foliage such
as grevillea
5 stems blue irises
5 stems white irises
10 stems daffodils
5 stems anemones ('Mona Lisa' blue)
concealing material such as broken
windscreen (windshield) glass

TIP
Glass has the advantage as a
concealing material – over pebbles
and granite, for example – of catch
ing and reflecting the light in an
attractive way.

1 Cut three short lengths of
florist's adhesive clay and press
on to the bottom of the pinholder.
Position this to one side of the
container and press firmly in place.

2 Define the shape of the "L" with
long, straight stems of foliage
placed at right angles to one another.
Note that the principal upright stem
is a little way in from the edge of the
pinholder. Give balance to the design
by placing a shorter stem to the left
of the principal stem with another
angled to the right.

3 Position the irises, pressing the
stems firmly on to the pinholder
spikes, so that the flowers follow the
shape outlined by the leaves.

4 Position the daffodils to fill in the gaps and complement the contrasting shape of the irises. Place a cluster of short-stemmed anemones close to the pinholder, where the flowers will be seen as deep shadows, and add a few foliage sprays. Spoon the concealing material – in this case broken windscreen (windshield) glass – around the pinholder until it is completely hidden.

OLD-FASHIONED GARDEN ROSE ARRANGEMENT

The beautiful full-blown blooms of these antique-looking roses give an opulent and romantic feel to a very simple combination of flower and container. This arrangement deserves centre stage in any room setting.

MATERIALS

*watertight container, to put inside
plant pot
low, weathered terracotta plant pot
jug (pitcher)
variety garden roses, short- and
long-stemmed
scissors*

TIP

The technique is to mass one type of flower in several varieties whose papery petals will achieve a textural mix of colour and scent.

1 Place the watertight container inside the terracotta plant pot and fill with water. Fill the jug (pitcher) as well. Select and prepare your blooms and remove the lower foliage and thorns.

2 Position the longer-stemmed blooms in the jug (pitcher) with the heads massed together. This ensures that the cut stems are supported and so can simply be placed directly into the water.

3 Mass shorter, more open flower heads in the glass bowl inside the plant pot with the stems hidden and the heads showing just above the rim of the pot. The heads look best if kept either all on one level or in a slight dome shape. If fewer flowers are used, plastic-coated wire mesh netting or plastic foam may be needed to control the positions of individual blooms.

SUMMER BASKET DISPLAY

*The lovely scents, luscious blooms and vast range of colours
available in summer provide endless possibilities for creating wonderful displays.
This arrangement is a bountiful basket, overflowing with seasonal summer
blooms, which can be scaled up or down to suit any situation.*

MATERIALS

*basket
cellophane (plastic wrap)
scissors
2 blocks plastic foam
florist's adhesive tape
10 stems Viburnum tinus
15 stems larkspur in 3 colours
6 stems 'Stargazer' lilies
5 large ivy leaves
10 stems white phlox*

1 Line the basket with cellophane (plastic wrap) to prevent leakage, and cut to fit. Then secure the two soaked blocks of plastic foam in the lined basket with the florist's adhesive tape.

2 Arrange the viburnum stems in the plastic foam to establish the overall height, width and shape. Strengthen the outline using the larkspur, making sure you use all of the stems and not just the flower spikes.

TIP

Keep the display well watered and it should go on flowering for at least a week. The lilies should open fully in plastic foam and new phlox buds will keep opening to replace the spent heads.

3 Place the lilies in a diagonal line across the arrangement. Position the large ivy leaves around the lilies in the centre of the display. Arrange the phlox across the arrangement along the opposite diagonal to the lilies.

ALL FOLIAGE ARRANGEMENT

*Creating an arrangement entirely from different types of foliage can be
both challenging and rewarding. No matter what the season, finding three
or four varieties of foliage is not difficult. Anything from the common
privet to the most exotic shrubs can be used and to great effect.*

MATERIALS

2 blocks plastic foam
large shallow bowl
florist's adhesive tape
scissors
stub (floral) wires
bun moss
5 stems grevillea
10 stems shrimp plant
(Beloperone guttata)
10 stems ming fern
(cultivar of Boston fern)
10 stems Pittosporum
5 stems cotoneaster

1 Soak the plastic foam and secure
it in the bowl with florist's
adhesive tape.

2 Make U-shaped staples from
stub (floral) wire and pin bun
moss around the rim of the bowl.

3 Arrange the grevillea to establish
the maximum height. Work
diagonally across with progressively
shorter stems, finishing with foliage
flowing over the front of the bowl.
Arrange the shrimp plant in a similar
way along the opposite diagonal, but
make it shorter than the grevillea and
emphasize the line by adding ming fern.

4 Intersperse the line of grevillea
with the *Pittosporum*. Finally,
distribute the cotoneaster evenly
throughout the whole arrangement.

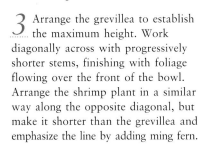

COUNTRY STYLE

A medley of cottage-garden flowers vividly contrasting in shape,
texture, and colour are arranged just as they might grow in a border –
intermingled and in profusion.

MATERIALS

plastic-coated wire
mesh netting
large jug (pitcher) or vase
florist's adhesive tape
scissors
3 stems Euphorbia fulgens
15 stems goldenrod
6 stems delphiniums
9 stems marigolds

1 Crumple the wire mesh netting into a ball and fit it into the neck of the jug (pitcher) so that it forms a mound above the rim. Criss-cross two pieces of adhesive tape over the wire, threading them through it in places and sticking the ends to the container. Arrange the arched stems of *Euphorbia* so that they droop over the jug handle, on one side only.

2 Arrange the goldenrod stems so that they form a pyramid shape, with the tallest ones in the centre.

3 Position the delphinium stems among the goldenrod and towards the back of the design.

4 Arrange the round, flat-faced marigold flowers at varying heights so that they are seen in a circular formation. Select the best, brightest specimen to place in the centre front, where it will overlap the rim of the jug.

BLUE AND WHITE TUSSIE MUSSIES

*Small, hand-tied spiralled posies make perfect gifts and, in the right vase,
ideal centre decorations for small tables. Both of these displays have
delicate flowers massed together. One features Japanese anemones,
visually strengthened by blackberries on stems; the other delphiniums
supported by rosehip stems.*

MATERIALS

TUSSIE 1 (ON LEFT)
10 stems white Japanese anemones
blackberries on stems
1 stem draceana
twine
scissors
ribbon

TUSSIE 2 (ON RIGHT)
4-5 stems 'Blue Butterfly' delphiniun
3 stems rosehips
5 small Virginia creeper leaves
twine
scissors
ribbon

1 Start with a central flower and add stems of foliage and flowers, turning the posy in your hand to build the design into a spiral.

2 Once all the ingredients have been used, and the bunch is completed, tie firmly at the binding point with twine. Repeat steps one and two for the second tussie mussie.

3 Trim the ends of the flower stems with scissors to achieve a neat edge. Finish both tussie mussies with ribbon bows.

*T*IP

While the flowers need to be tightly massed for the best effect, they have relatively lárge but fragile blooms, so take care nót to crush their petals, and tie off firmly but gently.

AUTUMN CROCUS TRUG

Bring the outdoors inside by planting up an old trug with flowering crocus bulbs in soil covered in a natural-looking carpet of moss and leaves. This simple display is as effective as the most sophisticated cut-flower arrangement.

trug
cellophane (plastic wrap)
soil
6 flowering crocus bulbs
bun moss
autumn leaves
raffia
scissors

1 Line the trug with cellophane (plastic wrap), fill with soil and plant the crocus bulbs. Ensure the bulbs are firmly planted and then water them.

2 Arrange the bun moss on top of the soil, then scatter the leaves over the moss to create a natural-looking, autumnal effect.

TIP

Although one expects to see crocuses in the spring, this beautiful autumn variety is a welcome sight as its flowers push up determinedly through the fallen leaves. Of course, they do not have to be confined to the garden.

3 To finish, tie raffia into bows, and attach one on either side of the base of the trug handle.

WHITE JAPANESE ANEMONE VASE

This delightful arrangement combining forest fruits and rosehips with garden anemones, though simple in concept, becomes a sumptuous display when placed in this elegant vase.

MATERIALS

vase
scissors
blackberries on stems
rosehips on stems
2 stems white Japanese anemones
'Honorine Jobert'
4 vine leaves

1 Having filled the vase with water, use the blackberry stems to establish the outline shape. Add the stems of rosehips to reinforce both the structure and the visual balance of the display.

2 Add the anemones evenly throughout the arrangement. Take great care with anemones as they are extremely delicate.

TIP
The rosehips and blackberry stalks used here are very prickly; they need careful handling and the thorns need to be stripped. However, these stems form a strong framework to hold the delicate anemones in position. The addition of vine leaves around the neck of the vase provides a finishing touch to the arrangement.

3 Place the stems of the vine leaves in the water so that they form a collar around the base of the arrangement and are visible above the neck of the vase.

ORANGE ARRANGEMENT

*The matt green of salal tips creates the perfect background for the
spectacular zesty orange colour of the flowers used in this display.*

MATERIALS

*wire basket
reindeer moss
cellophane (plastic wrap)
knife
1 block plastic foam
florist's adhesive tape
scissors
10 stems salal tips
7 stems orange lilies
10 stems orange tulips
20 stems marigolds*

1 Line the basket with reindeer
moss and line the moss with
cellophane (plastic wrap). Cut a
block of soaked plastic foam to fit
the basket and tape securely in place.

2 Push the salal tips into the
plastic foam to create a dome-
shaped foliage outline in proportion
with the container.

3 Cut the lily stems to a length to
suit the foliage framework and
push into the foam evenly throughout the arrangement to reinforce the
overall shape. Distribute the tulips
evenly through the display, remem-
bering they will continue to grow
and their natural downward curve
will tend to straighten.

4 Add the marigolds last and
place them evenly throughout
the display.

LILY AND HYACINTH PLANTED BASKET

When the budget is tight, an economic way of creating a large display
with lots of impact is to use plants instead of cut flowers.

MATERIALS

large wire basket
bun or carpet moss
cellophane (plastic wrap)
scissors
3 flowering lily plants (3 stems
per pot), such as 'Mona Lisa'
3 flowering hyacinth bulbs
8 red-barked dogwood (Cornus alba)
branches (or similar)
raffia

1 Line the whole basket with a layer of moss then, in turn, line the moss with cellophane (plastic wrap). Cut to fit.

2 Using the soil from their pots, plant the lilies in the lined basket, with the hyacinth bulbs between them. Cover the soil with moss.

TIP
The branches of the red-barked dogwood are tied with raffia to form a decorative and supportive structure around the arrangement. A more formal look can be achieved by substituting bamboo canes, tied perhaps with strips of velvet in rich colours.

3 Push four branches of dogwood through the moss and into the soil to form a square around the plants. Cross those horizontally with four more branches, tying them together with raffia to create a frame, then trim the raffia.

ARUM LILY VASE

*Pure in colour and form, elegant and stately, the arum lily has
the presence to be displayed on its own, supported by the minimum of
well-chosen foliage. Here it is arranged with the wonderfully
contorted willow and the large, simple leaves of aucuba, which serve
purely as a backdrop to the beauty of the arum.*

MATERIALS

vase
branches of contorted willow
scissors
6 arum lilies
2 bushy branches aucuba 'Gold Dust'

1 Fill the vase to approximately three-quarters full with water. Arrange the contorted willow in the vase to establish the overall height of the arrangement. (When cutting a willow stem to the right length, cut the base at a 45° angle and scrape the bark off to approximately 5 cm (2 in) from the end, then split this section.)

TIP

The choice of container is of great importance, the visual requirement being for simple unfussy shapes, with glass and metal being particularly appropriate. The chosen vase should complement the sculptural impact of the arum.

2 Arrange the arum lilies at different heights throughout the willow to achieve a visual balance. The willow stems will help support the blooms. Give visual substance to the display by adding stems of aucuba throughout to provide a dark backdrop to throw the arum blooms into sharp relief.

FRESH VALENTINE TERRACOTTA POTS

*With luck, Valentine's Day brings with it red roses, but these small
jewel-like arrangements present them in an altogether different way.
The deep red of the roses visually links the two pots: contrasting with the
acid lime green of 'Santini' chrysanthemums in one, and combining richly
with purple phlox in the other.*

MATERIALS

*half block plastic foam
2 small terracotta pots, 1 slightly
larger than the other
cellophane (plastic wrap)
knife
scissors
ming fern
ivy leaves
5 stems 'Santini' spray
chrysanthemums
6 stems purple phlox
18 stems dark red roses*

1 Soak the plastic foam in water. Line both terracotta pots with cellophane (plastic wrap). Cut the foam into small blocks and wedge into the lined pots. Then trim the cellophane to fit. Do not trim too close to the edge of the pot.

2 Build a dome-shaped foliage outline in proportion to each pot. In the larger pot, push the stems of ming fern into the plastic foam and in the small pot push the ivy leaves into the foam.

3 In the larger pot, arrange 'Santini' chrysanthemums amongst the ming fern. In the small pot, distribute the purple phlox amongst the ivy to emphasize the dome shapes of both.

4 Strip the leaves from the dark red roses, cut the stems to the desired lengths and arrange evenly throughout both displays.

DAFFODIL WOOD

*This Easter arrangement evokes one of the loveliest harbingers of spring –
the sight of golden daffodils making a bright floral carpet under the bare
branches of an apple tree. The arrangement could be positioned in
a church porch, on the floor, or on a low wooden chest.*

MATERIALS

*large flat plate
large flat woven tray, about
40 cm (16 in) diameter
scissors
florist's adhesive clay
2 plastic prongs
plastic foam, cut to size and
then soaked
knife
piece of well-shaped wood,
such as vinewood
stub (floral) wires
sphagnum moss
20 stems daffodils
30 stems narcissuses
10 ivy trails (sprigs)
5 short stems pussy willow
with catkins*

1 Place the plate or other solid waterproof liner in the tray. Cut two strips of adhesive clay and press them on to the underside of both plastic prongs. Press them in position well apart on the liner, where they will anchor the main blocks of foam. Press two large pieces of foam on to the spikes and cut other pieces to fill in the circle around the edges. Cut a hole in the foam, towards the back and at one side, and push the vinewood into it. Twist two or three wires around the wood, twist the ends and press them at different angles into the foam, so that the "tree" is held firmly in place.

TIP

If you are not fortunate enough to find a shapely piece of wood in the countryside, you could use a handful of gnarled twigs – apple would be ideal.

2 Cover the foam with a thin layer of moss. Scrape away just enough of the moss to expose small areas, and press the daffodil stems vertically into the foam. Cut them to slightly varying heights to give the most natural effect.

3 Cut shorter stems of narcissus and arrange them in a group in front of the daffodils. Position stems of ivy to twine around the vinewood and trail through a clump of daffodils. Position short sprays of ivy around the rim to edge and enclose the design and arrange a few pussy willow stems with catkins to provide shape and texture variation.

CELEBRATION TABLE DECORATION

A table for any celebratory lunch will not usually have much room
to spare on it. In this instance, there is no room for the wine cooler,
and the answer is to incorporate it within the flower arrangement.
The floral decoration is a sumptuous, textural display of gold, yellow
and white flowers with green and grey foliage.

MATERIALS

....

40 cm (16 in) diameter plastic
foam ring
scissors
12 stems Senecio laxifolius
15 stems elaeagnus
3 groups of 2 chestnuts
stub (floral) wires
thick gloves
18 stems yellow roses
10 stems cream-coloured
Eustoma grandiflorum
10 stems solidago
10 stems fennel

1 Soak the plastic foam ring in water. Cut the senecio to a stem length of around 14 cm (5½ in) and distribute evenly around the ring, pushing the stems into the plastic foam. Leave the centre of the ring clear.

3 Double leg mount three groups of two chestnuts on stub (floral) wire and cut the wire legs to about 6 cm (2¼ in). Take care, as the chestnuts are extremely prickly. It is advisable to wear thick gardening gloves when handling them. Position the chestnuts at three equidistant points around the circumference of the plastic foam ring, and secure by pushing the wires into the foam.

2 Cut the elaeagnus to a length of 14 cm (5½ in) and distribute evenly throughout the senecio to reinforce the foliage outline.

4 Cut the rose stems to about 14 cm (5½ in) in length and arrange in staggered groups of three roses at six points around the ring, equal distances apart, pushing the stems firmly into the foam.

5 Cut stems of eustoma flower heads 12 cm (4¾ in) long from the main stem. Arrange the stems evenly in the foam. Cut the stems of solidago to a length of about 14 cm (5½ in) and distribute throughout. Finally, cut the stems of fennel to about 12 cm (4¾ in) long and add evenly throughout the display.

SCENTED BASKET

*A young bridesmaid may find it easier to carry a basket than clutch a posy
during a seemingly endless wedding ceremony.
This basket uses simple flowers, in a simple colour combination,
simply arranged. The result is a beautiful display appropriate for
a child bridesmaid or a Mother's Day gift.*

MATERIALS

*small basket
cellophane (plastic wrap)
scissors
quarter block plastic foam
knife
florist's adhesive tape
ribbon
silver wires
20 10 cm (4 in) stems golden privet
6 stems tuberose
20 stems 'Grace' freesias*

1 Line the basket with cellophane (plastic wrap), and trim to fit. Soak the plastic foam in water, trim to fit into the basket, and secure in the centre with florist's adhesive tape. Form two small bows from the ribbon. Tie around their centres with silver wires and attach them to the basket, leaving the excess wire projecting at their back. Bind the handle of the basket with ribbon, securing it at either end by tying around the wire tails of the bows.

2 Build a domed outline to the arrangement with the golden privet, cut to the appropriate length.

3 Cut the tuberose stems to about 9 cm (3½ in) and position in a staggered diagonal across the basket.

4 Cut the freesia stems to around 9 cm (3½ in) long and space evenly throughout the basket. Recess some heads to give greater depth to the finished display.

TIED BRIDAL BOUQUET

*This classic "shower" wedding bouquet has a generous trailing shape
and incorporates* Lilium longiflorum *as its focal flowers, using the
traditional, fresh bridal colour combination of white, cream and green.*

MATERIALS

10 stems Lilium longiflorum
10 stems cream Eustoma grandiflorum
10 stems white Euphorbia fulgens
5 stems Molucella laevis
10 stems white aster 'Monte Cassino'
10 stems dill
10 ivy trails (sprigs)
twine
scissors
raffia

1 Hold one lily stem in your hand about 25 cm (10 in) down from the top of its flower head. Begin adding the other flowers and ivy trails (sprigs) in a regular sequence to get an even distribution of materials throughout the bouquet. As you do this, keep turning the bunch in your hand to make the stems form a spiral.

2 To one side of the bouquet add materials on longer stems than the central flower – these will form the trailing element of the display. To the opposite side, add stems slightly shorter than the central bloom, and this will become the top of the bouquet.

3 When you have finished the bouquet and are satisfied with the shape, tie it with twine at the binding point, firmly, but not too tightly. Cut the stems so that they are 12 cm (4¾ in) long below the binding point. Any shorter and the weight of the bouquet will not be distributed evenly and it will make it difficult to carry.

4 Tie raffia around the binding point and form a bow which sits on top of the stems, facing upwards towards the person carrying the bouquet.

TIP
A bouquet of this size requires quite a large quantity of material, which may prove expensive, but the design lends itself to being scaled down to suit a tighter budget by using the same materials in smaller quantities.

BABY BIRTH GIFT

*Celebrate a baby's birth by giving the parents this very pretty arrangement
in an unusual but practical container. The display incorporates double tulips,
ranunculus, phlox and spray roses, with small leaves of* Pittosporum. *It is the
delicacy of the flowers and foliage which make it appropriate for a baby.*

MATERIALS

*1 block plastic foam
knife
small galvanized metal bucket
scissors
1 bunch* Pittosporum
*15 stems pale pink 'Angelique' tulips
5 stems white spray roses
10 stems white ranunculus
10 stems white phlox
1 bunch dried lavender
ribbon*

TIP

The choice of soft subtle colours
means it is suitable for either a boy
or girl. There is also the added
bonus of the beautiful scent of phlox
and dried lavender.

2 Cut the 'Angelique' tulips to a
stem length of 10 cm (4 in) and
distribute them evenly throughout the
foliage. Cut individual off-shoots
from the main stems of the spray
roses to a length of 10 cm (4 in), and
arrange throughout the display, with
full blooms at the centre and buds
around the outside.

1 Soak the plastic foam in water,
cut it to fit the small metal
bucket and wedge it firmly in place.
Cut the *Pittosporum* to a length of
12 cm (4¾ in) and clean the leaves
from the lower part of the stems.
Push the stems into the plastic foam
to create an overall domed foliage
outline within which the flowers can
be arranged.

3 Cut the ranunculus and phlox to
a stem length of 10 cm (4 in)
and distribute both throughout the
display. Cut the lavender to a stem
length of 12 cm (4¾ in) and arrange
in groups of three stems evenly
throughout the flowers and foliage.
Tie the ribbon around the bucket
and finish in a generous bow.

GOLDEN WEDDING BOUQUET

*This shimmering bouquet makes an unequivocal Golden Wedding
statement. Unashamed in its use of yellows and golds, the colours are
carried right through the design in the flowers, the wrapping paper,
the twine and the ribbon, even to a fine sprinkling of gold dust.*

MATERIALS

*20 stems golden yellow ranunculus
20 stems mimosa
gold twine
scissors
2 sheets gold-coloured tissue paper
in 2 shades
piece gold-coloured fabric
about 46 cm (18 in) long,
15 cm (6 in) wide
gold dust glitter*

1 Lay out the stems of ranunculus
and mimosa so that they are
easily accessible. Clean the stems of
leaves from about a third of the way
down. Holding a stem of ranunculus
in your hand, build the bouquet by
adding alternate stems of mimosa
and ranunculus, turning the flowers
in your hand all the while so that the
stems form a spiral.

TIP
The arrangement makes a flamboyant gift but nonetheless is as simple
to create as a hand-tied bouquet.
It can be unwrapped and placed
straight into a vase of water, with
no need for further arranging.

2 When all the flowers have been
arranged in your hand, tie the
stems together at the binding point
with the gold twine. When secured,
trim the stems to a length about
one-third of the overall height of
the finished bouquet.

3 Wrap the bouquet in two shades
of tissue paper, and tie the gold
twine around the binding point.
Then tie a bow of gold fabric around
the binding point. To finish, sprinkle
gold dust over the flowers.

PARTY PIECE

Flowers arranged for a buffet party or a special family celebration can use artistic licence in the matter of colour, break some of the rules and earn nothing but praise. This party piece proves that you can blend red, blue, orange, mauve, yellow and green – all the colours of the rainbow – in an arrangement that will command attention across a crowded room.

MATERIALS

florist's adhesive clay
1 plastic prong
footed glass or china dish such as a cake stand
plastic foam, soaked in water
scissors
10 stems foliage such as eucalyptus and grevillea
15 stems Peruvian lilies
6 stems Singapore orchids
5 stems blue irises
5 stems pale-coloured roses
6 stems mixed carnations

TIP

This is an occasion when you can give way to the temptation to choose several bunches of flowers of different types, colours, shapes and sizes. Cut all the stem ends at a sharp angle to facilitate the intake of water, and give the flowers a long drink in cool water before arranging them.

1 Stick a piece of adhesive clay to the underside of the plastic prong and press on to the container slightly behind the centre point. Press the soaked foam on to the spikes of the prong. Arrange the various types of foliage to make a fan shape across the centre of the arrangement, and to cascade down over the rim of the container at the front and sides.

2 Arrange the Peruvian lilies – here deep coral, peach and cream colours were used – to follow the outline of the foliage. Cut some of the individual flowers on short stems and position them close to the foam.

3 Arrange the orchid stems in a triangular shape throughout the design, the tallest stem upright in the centre and progressively shorter stems slanted outwards at the front. If you cut the stems short and have to cut off some of the lower florets, position these as attractive "fillers" close to the foam.

4 Arrange the irises to make a patch of contrasting colour – the only blue in the design – at the back. Cut the stems at a sharply slanting angle. The sword-like leaves can be used at the back of the arrangement. Turn the container around and fill in the back of the design with sprays of foliage and a selection of flowers to give the arrangement depth and perspective.

5 Complete the arrangement by adding the softening influence of the roses and carnations, which contrast well with the trumpet- and star-like shapes of the other flowers. Add more foliage to fill in any gaps, and check that the design looks good from both sides.

FIT FOR A BRIDE

*For a close friend or a relative of the bride it is both a pleasure and
a privilege to compose the bridal bouquet. Confirm her preference for
flower types and colours, then follow our easy step-by-step instructions for
a bouquet fit for the most discerning bride.*

MATERIALS

*stub (floral) wires
wire cutters
white floral tape
florist's silver roll wire
scissors
Singapore orchids
Peruvian lilies
freesias
irises
narcissus
roses
mimosa
ballota and pampas grass
satin ribbon*

1 It is essential to wire flowers for a bouquet of this kind, otherwise the bundle of stems forming the handle would both look and feel clumsy. Cut short the flower stems and push a stub (floral) wire into the ends. Bind over the join and down along the wire with overlapping white floral tape.

2 Gather together all the flowers that will form the centre of the bouquet – orchids, Peruvian lilies, freesias, irises, narcissus and a rose – and bind the false wire stems with silver roll wire.

3 Hold the core of the bouquet in one hand and arrange slender stems of foliage to cascade over the flowers. Arrange a second layer of flowers around the front and sides of the central ones and bind all the stems and false stems with silver roll wire.

TIP

Design the bride's bouquet to feature the flowers and colours that will set the scene for the ceremony and the reception and complement the colours she and her attendants will wear. If the bride's dress is in off-white or cream, avoid using pure white flowers which would be unflattering to the fabric. Give all the flowers a long drink of cool water in a shady place before composing the bouquet.

4 Arrange a third layer of flowers around the front and sides of the bouquet, bind the stems with silver roll wire, and add a few feature flowers close to the grip. Roses and short sprays of mimosa look good in this position. Bind the stems again with wire, and then with the satin ribbon, tying it just under the lowest of the flowers. Tie the ribbon in a bow and leave long, trailing ends. Spray the flowers with a fine mist of cool water, and keep in a cool place.

FRESH FLOWERS AS A GIFT-WRAP DECORATION

*This flower decoration offers the opportunity to make a gift extra special,
and to give flowers at the same time. The colour and form of the gerbera
and 'Mona Lisa' lily heads are very bold, and this is contrasted with the
small delicate bell heads of lily-of-the-valley.*

MATERIALS

*1 stem 'Mona Lisa' lily
scissors
1 branch lichen-covered larch
1 small pot lily-of-the-valley
2 stems pink gerbera
raffia
gift-wrapped present
ribbon*

1 From the lily stem, cut a 20 cm (8 in) length with one bud and one open flower on it. Also cut a single open flower on an 8 cm (3¼ in) stem. Cut six twigs from the larch branch, each about 25 cm (10 in) long. Cut three lily-of-the-valley on stems approximately 15 cm (6 in) long, each with a leaf. Cut one gerbera stem to 18 cm (7 in) long and the second to 14 cm (5½ in) long. Create a flat fan-shaped outline with the larch twigs. Position the longer lily stem in the centre of the fan and the shorter single one below.

Next arrange the lily-of-the-valley and gerbera around the two lilies. Tie the stems securely with raffia at the point where they all cross.

TIP

The decoration is made as a small, tied, flat-based sheaf. This involves no wiring and thus is relatively simple to make, provided you give sufficient thought to the visual balance between the bold and delicate elements.

2 Lay the completed decoration diagonally across the wrapped gift. Take a long piece of raffia around the flowers, crossing under the parcel and bringing it back up to tie off on top of the stems.

Wrap the ribbon around the binding point of the decoration and tie a bow.

WEDDING DECORATION

*Hanging decorations in a church or chapel complement the larger
arrangements, the pedestal and windowsill designs, and further enhance
the setting for a wedding or baptism. Such decorations may hang on the ends
of pews, or on pillars, posts and altar screens.*

MATERIALS

*small block plastic foam, soaked
in water
plastic foam-holding tray, with handle
florist's adhesive tape (optional)
4 stems grevillea
8 stems broom
a few stems variegated leaves and
flowering shrub
2 stems carnations
4-5 stems mixed irises
8-10 stems Peruvian lilies
2 stems white spray carnations
scissors
6 mm (¼ in) wide ribbon
stub (floral) wires
wire cutters
ribbon
wire or twine for hanging*

TIP

If making more than one decoration,
divide the flowers and foliage
into groups before you start the
arrangements, so that they all match
one another.

2 Cut short a carnation stem and
position it just above the centre
of the foam. Arrange the irises above
and below it. Cut individual Peruvian
lily flowers and arrange them to
form the background of the design.

1 Press a slice cut from a block
of soaked foam into the plastic
holder. Hold the container vertically,
and check that the foam is held
firmly in place. If necessary, tape it
in place with two strips of florist's
adhesive tape. Arrange long stems of
slender foliage at the top and bottom
of the holder and shorter sprays in
the centre.

3 Arrange sprays of foliage and
shrub to isolate some of the
flowers. Extend the outline with
spray carnations. Cut the narrow
ribbon into three lengths, double
each one, and tie into a bow. Thread
a stub (floral) wire through the back
of the loop and press into the foam.
Make 3 bows from the other ribbon
in the same way and position them
at the base of the decoration.

CHRISTMAS CANDLE TABLE DECORATION

*This rich display is a visual feast of the seasonal reds and greens of
anemones, ranunculus and holly, softened by the grey of lichen on
larch twigs and aromatic rosemary. The simple white candles are given
a festive lift with their individual bows.*

MATERIALS

*25 cm (10 in) diameter plastic
foam ring
25 cm (10 in) diameter
wire basket with candleholders
10 stems rosemary
10 small stems lichen-covered larch
10 small stems holly
scissors
30 stems red anemones ('Mona Lisa')
30 stems red ranunculus
paper ribbon
4 candles*

TIP

The space at the centre of the design
is the perfect spot for hiding those
little, last-minute surprise presents!

Never leave burning candles
unattended and do not allow the
candles to burn below 5 cm (2 in)
of the display height.

1 Soak the plastic foam ring in
water and wedge it snugly into
the wire basket. You may need to
trim the ring slightly, but make sure
that you do not cut too much off
by mistake.

2 Using a combination of
rosemary, larch and holly,
create an even but textured foliage
and twig outline, all around the
plastic foam ring. Make sure that the
various foliages towards the outside
edge of the display are shorter than
those towards the centre.

3 Cut the stems of the anemones
and ranunculus to 7.5 cm (3 in).
Arrange them evenly throughout the
display, leaving a little space around
the candleholders. Make four ribbon
bows and attach them to the candles.
Position the candles in the holders.

CHRISTMAS ANEMONE URN

This vibrant display uses fabulously rich colours as an alternative to the traditional reds and greens of Christmas. An audacious combination of shocking orange roses set against the vivid purple anemones and the metallic blue berries of laurustinus makes an unforgettable impression.

MATERIALS

1 small cast-iron urn
cellophane (plastic wrap)
1 block plastic foam
florist's adhesive tape
scissors
1 bunch laurustinus with berries
10 stems bright orange roses
20 stems anemones ('Mona Lisa' blue)

TIP

The classic feel of a Christmas arrangement is retained by the use of the rusting cast-iron urn in which this spectacular display is set.

1 Line the urn with the cellophane (plastic wrap). Soak the plastic foam in water, fit into the lined urn and secure with adhesive tape. Trim the cellophane (plastic wrap) to fit.

2 Clean the stems of laurustinus and evenly arrange in the plastic foam to create a domed, all-round foliage framework within which the flowers will be positioned.

3 Distribute the roses, the focal flowers, evenly throughout the foliage, placing those with the most open blooms about two-thirds of the way up the arrangement.

4 Push the stems of anemones into the plastic foam amongst the roses, spreading them throughout the arrangement so that a domed and regular shape is achieved.

Dried Flowers

There is a tremendous variety of material to choose from for dried flower arrangements. Instead of buying them ready-made, you can dry your own material at home, most simply by air-drying. The projects which follow, ranging from elegant, simple bouquets to exotic combinations, also feature displays for special occasions. Each one demonstrates how dried flowers are most effective when used in clusters.

WORKING WITH DRIED FLOWERS

The extensive range of dried materials available today makes it possible to enjoy the beauty of your favourite blooms throughout the year, as well as enabling you to experiment with new textures and colours by combining flowers with other materials. Many fresh flowers and plant materials can also be dried at home.

BUYING DRIED FLOWERS READY PREPARED

Many florists stock a wide range of dried, natural materials and will offer advice on combining colours and textures. They may even be able to order your materials specifically.

DRYING YOUR OWN FLOWERS

In order to prevent flowers from becoming too dry and lifeless, remove the moisture from the fresh flower or plant material quickly.

Air-drying is the simplest form of flower preservation, requiring no specialist materials or expertise. Moisture is removed from the petals simply by circulating air.

1 Ensure that the flowers are dry, with no residual moisture from rain or dew. Choose perfect specimens only, as imperfections look unsightly in preserved arrangements.

2 Remove any large leaves which shrivel when dried. Unwanted smaller leaves should be rubbed off before drying.

3 Hang flowers upside-down in a dark, airy place. Gather the stems into small bunches and fasten each with elastic (rubber) bands.

Hydrangeas and gypsophila respond well to an alternative method of drying. Place the hydrangea stems (which should be fully mature) in a container with 2.5 cm (1 in) of water, and then allow them to absorb the water fully. Once the water has been absorbed, dry them out as normal.

Wood and organic materials always give a natural, earthy appearance, which can be a more sober complement to a colourful arrangement. Tree bark comes in a variety of shapes and sizes. Other ideas to combine are driftwood, sponge or golden mushrooms and for autumn or winter arrangements, try adding pine cones and cinnamon sticks. Exotic fruits can also enhance a design.

Left: There are flowers, materials and fruits from every season available for drying.

MAXIMIZING LIFE SPAN

Dried arrangements will not last forever, around six months is the maximum before they begin to look faded. Extend the life of a display by keeping it out of sunlight and not allowing it to become damp. Prevent the build up of dust with an occasional hair-dryer blast and when new, spray with hair lacquer to help prevent seeds and petals dropping.

Below: With careful drying, materials effectively retain their original colour and form.

ADDITIONAL DRIED MATERIAL

Foliage and mosses provide wonderful filler material, setting off the main focal flowers beautifully. The many different varieties, in neutral and colourful shades, each offer something different.

Stunning arrangements can be based on foliage, try beech leaf branches punctuated with golds and splashes of copper, silvery-grey eucalyptus for an airy arrangement, blue pine sprigs for Christmas wreaths, or for an eastern look, meandering willow.

Moss is good for lining a container or hiding wire fixings supporting the structure. Sea moss, bun moss, lichen, sphagnum moss and carpet moss are all easy to obtain. The rounded form and velvety texture of bun moss is particularly attractive.

FIREPLACE DISPLAY

This is one of the very best projects for a beginner. It is an extremely
simple design to make. Even though this display is for a fireplace,
turn it occasionally so that it fades evenly.

wire cutters
chicken wire
basket
amaranthus
pink larkspur
pink and red roses
lavender

TIP

A fireplace display will tend to get
dustier than others. Clean with a
hair-dryer set on cold, and finish
with a soft brush. If some flowers
break with this treatment, you can
easily replace the damaged stems
without disturbing the whole display.

1 Cut a piece of chicken wire
approximately twice the surface
area of the basket. Scrunch it up and
push it into the basket, filling the
whole of the inside.

2 Starting with the amaranthus,
push the stems into the basket,
through the wire mesh to the
bottom. Use this material as the
filler, and cover most of the top of
the wire mesh, leaving space for the
other flowers.

3 Arrange the larkspur in the
spaces between the amaranthus.
Stand back from the display to check
that the balance is correct.

4 Add the roses and lavender.
Make sure to put some rose
heads low down at the front of the
basket for added interest. Place the
display on the floor and check that
the balance is correct from all angles.

A SIMPLE POT OF ROSES

A simple rose pot display can be made in single colours or, as here, with a combination. Make a matching pair to stand on a mantelpiece or shelf for a symmetrical, formal effect, or perhaps add a fabric bow for a softer, more romantic appearance.

MATERIALS

knife
1 block plastic foam for dried flowers
terracotta pot
scissors
30 stems mixed roses
fresh moss
stub (floral) wires
wire cutters
glue gun (optional)

TIP
If you are using more than one colour, ensure that you have a good mix of hues over the display.

1 Trim the foam to fit the pot tightly and push in. Trim the top of the foam if necessary so that it is level with the top of the pot.

2 Trim each rose stem to the required length as you work. However, try to retain as much of the green leaf as possible.

3 Start in the middle of the foam, pressing in the tallest rose. Then work outwards, continuing to add the stems one by one. The roses should be at different levels so that the heads do not crowd each other.

4 Continue to press flowers into the pot. Finally, fix moss around the base of the roses with a glue gun. Alternatively, bend short stub (floral) wires to form U-shaped staples and push them into the foam to trap the moss.

CANDLE POT DISPLAY

This beautiful arrangement of dried flowers in a terracotta pot is designed to incorporate a candle. Contemporary in its use of massed flower heads, the display has the stunning colour combination of deep pink peonies and bright blue globe thistles surrounding a dark green candle and finished with a lime green ribbon. It would make a wonderful gift.

MATERIALS

knife
1 block plastic foam for dried flowers
terracotta pot, 15 cm (6 in) diameter
wide candle
10 stems deep pink peonies
15 stems small blue globe thistles
scissors

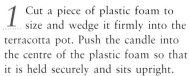

1 Cut a piece of plastic foam to size and wedge it firmly into the terracotta pot. Push the candle into the centre of the plastic foam so that it is held securely and sits upright.

2 Cut the peony stems to 4 cm (1½ in) and the globe thistle stems to 5 cm (2 in). First, push the stems of the peonies into the foam, followed by the globe thistle stems.

TIP
The effect of this display relies on the peonies being tightly massed together. Never leave burning candles unattended and do not allow the candles to burn below 5 cm (2 in) of the display height.

3 Ensure that the heads of all the flowers are at the same level. Wrap a ribbon around the top of the terracotta pot and tie it in a bow at the front. Shape the ends of the ribbon to avoid fraying.

SPICY STAR WALL DECORATION

*This star-shaped wall decoration is constructed from groups of long cinnamon
sticks. It is embellished with bunches of lavender to add colour, texture, contrast
and a scent which mixes with the warm, spicy smell of the construction.*

MATERIALS

*15 cinnamon sticks, 30 cm (12 in) long
raffia
scissors
75 stems lavender
ribbon*

1 Separate the cinnamon sticks into
five groups of three. Interlace the
ends of two groups of sticks to form
a point and secure firmly by tying
them together with raffia. Trim the
ends of the raffia.

2 Continue interlacing and binding
together groups of cinnamon
sticks to create a neat star-shaped
framework. Also, bind together the
sticks where they cross each other, to
make the frame rigid.

TIP
For a Christmas look, substitute
dried fruit slices and gilded seedheads
for the lavender. Similarly, any
sturdy straight twigs can be used
instead of the cinnamon.

3 Separate the lavender into five
bunches of 15 stems each. Turn
the star shape so that the binding
knots are at the back and attach the
bunches of lavender to the front of
the frame, using raffia at the cross
points of the cinnamon sticks.

4 When all the lavender bunches
have been secured, make a small
bow from the ribbon and tie it to the
decoration at the bottom crossing
point of the cinnamon sticks.

LOVE AND KISSES COLLAGE

This witty natural collage is made from tropical seedheads
and cinnamon sticks mounted on linen muslin. Even the frame has been
decorated with giant cinnamon sticks, glued over a simple wooden one.

MATERIALS

wooden picture frame
brown backing paper
scissors
linen muslin
glue gun
knife
small cinnamon sticks
florist's silver roll wire
heart-shaped or any other large
tropical seedheads
4 giant cinnamon sticks

1 Take the glass out of the picture frame and stick the backing paper to the hardboard backing. Cut the linen muslin to size, and fray the edges. Put spots of glue all around the edge of the muslin and then stick it to the backing.

2 Glue six short lengths of cinnamon into three crosses, and then wire them up to form a delicate metallic cross joint.

3 Glue the heart-shaped seedheads to the top of the picture; glue the cinnamon "kisses" to the bottom.

4 Finish by making a cinnamon-stick frame. Cut two giant cinnamon sticks to the same length as the frame and two to the same as the width. First glue a stick to the top of the frame, and then one to the bottom. Next, glue the side ones to these.

EVERLASTING BASKET

*Hydrangeas look fabulous dried, providing a flamboyant display that can
simply be massed into a basket. They're also about the easiest flowers to dry
at home. Just put the cut flowers in about 1 cm (½ in) of water and leave
them. The flowers will take up the water and then gradually dry out.*

MATERIALS

knife
1 block plastic foam for dried flowers
painted wooden basket
mop-head hydrangeas
globe artichokes
ribbon

1 Cut the plastic foam block to fit
and fill the basket, and then
arrange the hydrangeas to cover the
top of the basket.

2 Add the dried globe artichokes at
one end for texture.

3 Tie a ribbon to the handle of the
basket to finish.

FLOWER CONE

This unusual design employs a series of stacked rings around a cone shape,
each ring containing massed flowers of one type and colour to create a
quirky display with a strong geometric pattern.

MATERIALS

1 plastic foam cone for dried flowers,
28 cm (11 in) high
galvanized metal container,
approximately 11 cm (4½ in) diameter
scissors
20 stems floss flower
40 stems pink roses
20 stems marjoram
10 stems small globe thistle heads
ribbon

1 Wedge the plastic foam cone firmly into the galvanized container. Cut the floss flower stems to about 2.5 cm (1 in) long and arrange a ring around the bottom of the cone to follow the ellipse of the rim of the container. Cut the rose stems to about 2.5 cm (1 in) long and, tight to the first ring, arrange a second ring with the rose heads.

2 Cut the stems of the marjoram and globe thistle to about 2.5 cm (1 in). Tight to the ring of rose heads, form a third elliptical ring with the marjoram. Tight to the marjoram, form a fourth elliptical ring with the globe thistle. Repeat this sequence of rings until the whole cone is covered. At the tip, fix a single rose head. To finish, wrap the ribbon around the galvanized metal container and tie a small bow at the front of the display.

LAVENDER BLUE

The heady scent of lavender makes it a perfect component for a ring to display in a bedroom, a bathroom, beside a window seat, or wherever there is a hint of romance. A smaller ring could hang inside a wardrobe or over a decorative coathanger.

MATERIALS

48–60 stems lavender
scissors
florist's silver roll wire
yellow rosebuds
strawflowers
blue cornflowers
yellow lady's mantle
yellow sea lavender
gypsophila
glue gun
1 twig wreath
satin ribbon
3 stub (floral) wires

1 Gather eight or ten lavender stems into a bunch, cut short the stems and bind them with florist's wire. Make six mixed posies with the other dried flowers, arranging the full, rounded flowers like roses, strawflowers and cornflowers in the centre and the wispy sprays at the sides. Bind the stems with wire.

2 Run a thin strip of glue along the stems of the first lavender bunch and press on to the wreath. Stick on more bunches of lavender, the heads of each successive one covering the stems of the one before. At desired intervals, add the mixed posies in the same way.

3 Cut six equal lengths of ribbon, tie each into a bow and trim the ends. Cut the stub (floral) wires in half and bend to make U-shaped staples. Press five ribbon bows into the inside of the wreath and one on top. Glue on extra strawflower heads to fill any gaps or hide visible wires. Adjust the ribbon bows so they hang neatly and evenly.

TIP

For the posies, which are to alternate with the lavender bunches, choose flowers in soft, complementary colours – blue, cream and green are ideal. If a glue gun is not available, fix the bunches and posies to the wreath form with stub (floral) wires bent into U-shaped staples.

DUTCH INFLUENCE

Inspired by the magnificent paintings of the Dutch Masters, this arrangement is composed in a painted and gilded wooden urn. A cluster of fruits – pineapple, grapes, and pomegranates – and a jug (pitcher) of wine complete the luxurious quality of the still-life group.

MATERIALS

plastic-coated wire mesh netting
urn-shaped container
scissors
florist's adhesive tape
larkspur
deep pink, pale pink and cream roses
carnations
hydrangeas
long foliage
statice
strawflowers
lady's mantle

1 Crumple the wire mesh netting and place it in the neck of the vase. Tuck in any stray ends. Cut short lengths of adhesive tape, twist them around the wire at intervals, and stick them to the rim of the container. When the design has been completed, the tape will be covered by the shortest of the flowers. Position the larkspur stems to create a fan shape.

2 Build up one side of the design. Arrange the roses among the larkspur stems. Cut the stems in graduated lengths and position some roses close to the rim.

3 Build up the other side in a similar way. Position the full, rounded flowers, such as carnations and clusters of hydrangeas, close to the base. This gives visual weight to the design. Add sprays of dried foliage to create a variety of texture, and to give the arrangement a more natural look. Finally, complete the arrangement by filling in all the gaps with statice, strawflowers and lady's mantle until it has a generous and opulent overall appearance.

DECORATED POT DISPLAY

*This display is purely for fun. The container is a terracotta pot decorated
with a painted head against a bright blue background. You can decorate
a terracotta pot with your own design and create a complementary
floral display for it.*

MATERIALS

*knife
1 block plastic foam for dried flowers
hand-painted terracotta plant pot
florist's adhesive tape
stub (floral) wires
reindeer moss
scissors
20 stems small globe thistles
20 bleached cane spirals
30 stems white roses*

1 Cut the block of plastic foam so
that it wedges into the decorated
pot and extends approximately 4 cm
(1½ in) above the rim. Secure it in
place with florist's adhesive tape.
Make U-shaped staples from the stub
(floral) wires. Tuck reindeer moss
between the sides of the pot and the
plastic foam and push the wire
staples through the moss and into the
foam to secure.

2 Cut the globe thistle stems to
approximately 10 cm (4 in) in
length and arrange them throughout
the plastic foam to create an even,
domed shape.

3 Cut the cane spirals to a length
of about 15 cm (6 in) and push
their stems into the plastic foam,
distributing them evenly throughout
the globe thistles.

4 Cut the stems of the dried roses
to approximately 10 cm (4 in)
in length and arrange them evenly
amongst the other materials in
the display.

BATHROOM DISPLAY

The starfish in this arrangement evoke images of the sea,
while the soft pastel colours – shell pink, apricot, blue, pale green
and cream – give it a soft summer look.

MATERIALS
....

knife
2 blocks plastic foam for dried flowers
pale-coloured wooden trug
florist's adhesive tape
scissors
50 stems natural phalaris
40 stems shell-pink roses
20 stems cream-coloured strawflowers
150 stems lavender
15 small dried starfish
stub (floral) wires

1 Cut the block of plastic foam to fit the wooden trug and secure it in place with adhesive tape. Cut the individual stems of phalaris to a length of approximately 10 cm (4 in) and push them into the plastic foam to establish the height, width and overall shape of the arrangement.

2 Cut the stems of the dried roses to a length of approximately 10 cm (4 in) and push them into the plastic foam, distributing them evenly throughout.

TIP
Although a steamy environment will cause dried flowers to deteriorate, if you accept the shorter life span, such arrangements will add an attractive decorative feature to a bathroom.

3 Cut the strawflower stems to a length of about 10 cm (4 in) and push them into the foam amongst the roses and phalaris, recessing some. Cut the dried lavender to a length of 11 cm (4½ in) and, by pushing into the foam, arrange it throughout the display in groups of five stems.

4 Wire all the starfish individually by double leg mounting one of the arms with a stub (floral) wire. Cut the wire legs of the starfish to a length of about 10 cm (4 in) and push the wires into the foam, distributing them evenly throughout the display.

DESIGNER TREE

*Blossoming with strong primary colours set off by crisp white,
this indoor tree makes a natural link between the garden and the home,
and looks equally good in a doorway, on a windowsill, or a table.*

MATERIALS

florist's adhesive clay
1 plastic prong
painted earthenware flower pot,
about 12.5 cm (5 in) diameter
modelling or self-hardening clay,
or plaster of Paris
straight but branched twig, such as
apple wood
2 dry foam balls, 7.5 cm (3 in)
diameter
secateurs (pruning shears)
statice
blue sea lavender
red broom bloom
red rosebuds
cornflowers
strawflowers
checked ribbon
dry sphagnum moss

1 Press a strip of adhesive clay on to the base of the plastic prong, fix it in the base of the pot and push a ball of modelling or self-hardening clay firmly on to it. Insert the twig and press the clay around it to hold it in place. Push the dry foam balls on to the twig.

2 Cut short the flower stems – the shorter they are, the fewer you will need to cover the balls and conceal the foam. Cover the first sphere with stems of white statice alternated with blue sea lavender and cornflowers. Fill any remaining gaps with extra flowers.

TIP
To give this display a lighter look, the terracotta pot was painted with white emulsion (latex) paint.

3 Cover the second sphere in a
similar way, using short stems
of statice close to the foam and
longer, wispy red flowers to provide
a softer outline. Position a few rosebuds and strawflowers at intervals
among the statice. Tie a ribbon bow
just below the higher ball. To finish,
tie more ribbons close to the pot, to
trail over the rim. Instead of a multi-
coloured check design, narrow ribbon
or tape in each of the three principal
flower colours may be used. Cover
the holding material in the pot with
dry moss.

ROSE AND LAVENDER POSY

*A bouquet always makes a welcome gift, but a bunch of carefully selected
and beautifully arranged dried flowers will long outlast fresh blooms,
to become an enduring reminder of a happy occasion.*

MATERIALS

*stub (floral) wires
12 large artificial or glycerined leaves
florist's (stem-wrap) tape
1 bunch lavender
1 bunch rosebuds
florist's silver roll wire (optional)
paper ribbon*

1 Fold a stub (floral) wire one-third of the way along its length, to form a 15 cm (6 in) stalk. Attach a leaf to the top by its stalk, and bind in place with florist's (stem-wrap) tape, pulling and wrapping the tape down to the end of the wire. Repeat the process with all 12 leaves.

2 Divide the lavender into several small bunches. Hold them together loosely, setting the bunches at an angle to give a good shape. This will form the basic structure of the posy.

3 Taking a single rosebud at a time, push the stems into the lavender, spacing them out evenly.

4 If desired, bind the posy with florist's silver roll wire so it will keep its shape while you work. Then edge the posy with the wire-mounted leaves. Bind in place again.

5 Unravel the paper ribbon and use to bind all the stalks together tightly, covering the wire and the stalks completely. Finish off by tying the ends of the ribbon into a bow.

WALL HANGING SHEAF

The rustic charm of this delightful hand-tied sheaf is difficult to resist
especially since it is so easy to make once you have mastered the
ever-useful stem-spiralling technique.

MATERIALS

1 bunch linseed
1 bunch white strawflowers
10 stems carthamus
8 stems large orange-dyed globe thistles
10 stems green amaranthus (straight)
twine
scissors
green paper ribbon

TIP

The sheaf shape makes a feature of the stems as well as the blooms. Finished with a green ribbon, this decoration would look lovely hung in a country-style kitchen.

1 Set out the materials so that they are easily accessible. Divide each of the bunches of linseed and strawflowers into 10 smaller bunches. Break off the side shoots from the main stems of the carthamus and the globe thistles to increase the number of individual stems available. Take the longest stem of amaranthus in your hand and, to either side of it, add a stem of carthamus and a bunch of linseed, making sure all the material is slightly shorter than the amaranthus. The stems of the materials should be spiralled as they are added. Add materials to the bunch to maintain a visual balance between the bold forms of the globe thistles and strawflowers and the more delicate linseed and carthamus.

2 When all the materials have been incorporated, tie with twine at the binding point. Trim the ends of the stems.

3 Make a paper ribbon bow and attach it to the sheaf at the binding point with its tails pointing towards the flower heads.

SPICY POMANDER

Pomanders were originally nature's own air fresheners. The traditional orange pomanders are fairly tricky to do, because the critical drying process can so easily go wrong, leading to mouldy oranges. This one made of cloves and cardamom pods avoids the problem, and makes a refreshing change in soft, muted colours.

MATERIALS

cloves
1 dry foam ball, 7.5 cm (3 in) diameter
glue gun
green cardamom pods
raffia
1 stub (floral) wire

1 Start by making a single line of cloves all around the ball's circumference. Make another one in the other direction, so you have divided the ball into quarters.

2 Make a line of cloves on both sides of original lines to create broad bands of cloves quartering the ball.

3 Starting at the top of the first quarter, glue cardamom pods over the foam, methodically working in rows to create a neat effect. Repeat on the other three quarters.

4 Tie a bow in the centre of a length of raffia. Pass a stub (floral) wire through the knot and twist the ends together.

5 Fix the bow to the top of the
ball using the stub (floral) wire.
Join the two loose ends in a knot to
hang the pomander.

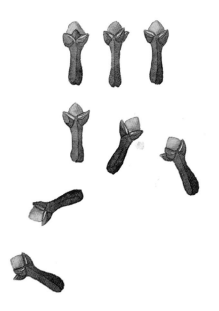

TRADITIONAL TIERED BASKET

*This regimented formal design can be very effective and is one of the
easiest for beginners to perfect. So long as you make sure that each layer
of materials is the correct height, you should make a dramatic display,
the loose and flowing ingredients combining well within the confines of
a disciplined structure.*

MATERIALS

*knife
1 block plastic foam for dried flowers
rectangular basket
wheat
stub (floral) wires
lavender
roses
fresh moss
scissors or cutters*

1 Cut the dry foam block to fill
the basket and press firmly in.
Start in the centre of the foam with
the wheat, the tallest ingredient,
wired into bunches of 8–10 stems.
Pack the stems closely together to
achieve a good density. Check that
the height of the wheat balances
with the basket size.

2 Wire the lavender into small
bunches of 5–6 stems and push
them into the foam directly in front
of the wheat. Arrange the stems so
that the lavender flowers come to
just below the heads of wheat. Make
sure the flowers are all facing the
same way to achieve a symmetry.

3 Add the roses next, positioning
them in front of the lavender.
Add the stems individually, and try
to keep as much foliage as space will
allow. Place the roses at slightly
varying heights to ensure that each
flower head is visible.

4 Complete the display by covering
the foam at the base with moss.
Fix this in place with stub (floral)
wires bent into U-shaped staples.
Fresh moss shrinks a little when it
dries, so allow it to overhang the
sides of the basket at this stage.

PEONY AND APPLE TABLE ARRANGEMENT

This delicate arrangement can be made for a specific occasion and kept to be used again and again, whenever a special arrangement is called for. The construction of the decoration is relatively simple, involving the minimum of wiring.

MATERIALS

knife
1 block plastic foam for dried flowers
terracotta bowl
florist's adhesive tape
scissors
10 stems preserved (dried) eucalyptus
18 slices preserved (dried) apple
stub (floral) wires
2 large heads hydrangea
10 stems pale pink peonies
20 stems deep pink roses
20 peony leaves
10 stems ti tree

1 Cut the block of plastic foam so that it wedges into the bowl and secure it in place with the florist's adhesive tape. Cut the eucalyptus stems to about 13 cm (5 in), making sure that the cut ends are clean of leaves, and arrange them evenly around the plastic foam to create a domed foliage outline to the display.

2 Group the slices of preserved (dried) apple into threes and double leg mount them with stub (floral) wires. Push the six groups of wired apple slices into the foam, distributing them evenly throughout the display.

3 Break each hydrangea head into three smaller florets and push them into the foam, distributing them evenly throughout the display, and recessing them slightly as you work.

4 Cut the stems of the peonies to approximately 12 cm (4¾ in) in length and arrange them evenly throughout the display. This time, the peonies should not be recessed.

5 Cut the dried rose stems to approximately 12 cm (4¾ in) in length and push them into the plastic foam throughout the other materials.

6 Arrange the dried peony leaves evenly amongst the flowers. Cut the ti tree into stems of approximately 12 cm (4¾ in) in length and distribute them throughout the display.

AUTUMN ROSE BUNDLE

*Roses, especially yellow or orange ones, will keep their colour for a very
long time, so this makes an ideal display to fill a dark corner.
For a smarter look, the arrangement could be trimmed with a fabric bow.*

MATERIALS

*1 cylinder plastic foam for
dried flowers
brown paper
glue gun
craft knife or scalpel
stub (floral) wires
pliers
scissors
12 stems orange or yellow roses
4 cobra leaves
raffia
fresh moss*

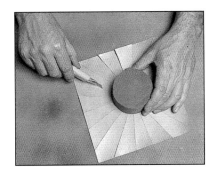

1 Place the foam cylinder in the
centre of the brown paper and
glue it in place. Cut from the edge of
the foam to the outer edge of the
paper, working all the way around at
roughly 1 cm (½ in) intervals.

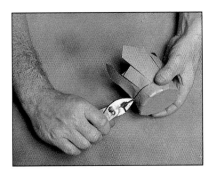

2 Fold the paper strips up to wrap
the foam. Wrap a stub (floral)
wire round the paper and the foam,
making sure all the paper strips are
straight at the base, and twist the
two ends of the wire tightly together.

3 Trim the paper in line with the
top of the foam. Cut the rose
stems, retaining as many leaves as
possible. Starting in the centre, push
them carefully into the foam.

4 Wrap three to four cobra leaves
around the base, fixing each one
in place with a U-shaped staple made
from a bent stub (floral) wire.

5 Wrap a stub (floral) wire around the leaves at the same level as the U-shaped staples and twist the ends tightly together to make a secure fixing. Trim the leaves at the base of the display with scissors, so that it will stand evenly.

6 Tie raffia round the base, covering all the fixings, and finish with a bow or a simple knot. If the roses had a limited number of leaves, fill the spaces around the stems with moss, to hide the foam.

AUTUMNAL ORANGE DISPLAY

Warm autumn colours dominate this display both in the flowers and the container. The lovely bulbous terracotta pot is a feature of the display, and the arrangement is domed to reflect the roundness of the container.

MATERIALS

3 blocks plastic foam for dried flowers
terracotta pot, 30 cm (12 in) high
florist's adhesive tape
10 stems glycerined adiantum
stub (floral) wires
9 dried split oranges
scissors
10 stems carthamus
10 stems orange-dyed globe thistles
10 stems bottlebrush

1 Pack the blocks of plastic foam into the terracotta pot and secure in place with florist's adhesive tape. The surface of the foam should be 4 cm (1¼ in) above the pot's rim.

2 Create a low domed outline with foliage using the adiantum stems at a length of about 25 cm (10 in). Wire the dried oranges with stub (floral) wire.

3 Bend down the wires projecting from the bases of the oranges and twist together. Arrange the oranges throughout the adiantum using their wire stems.

4 Cut the carthamus stems to approximately 25 cm (10 in) and push them into the plastic foam throughout the display to reinforce the height, width and overall shape.

5 Cut the globe thistle and bottle-brush stems to a length of approximately 25 cm (10 in) and push them into the foam evenly throughout the display.

SPICE TOPIARY

Fashion a delightfully aromatic, culinary topiary from cloves and star anise, put it in a terracotta pot decorated with cinnamon sticks and top with a cinnamon-stick cross. Sticking all the cloves into the florist's foam is both easy to do and wonderfully therapeutic.

MATERIALS

small "long Tom" terracotta
flowerpot
knife
cinnamon sticks
glue gun
1 plastic foam cone for dried flowers,
23 cm (9 in) tall
1 small plastic foam cone
stub (floral) wires
large pack of star anise
cloves

TIP

This lovely topiary would make an ideal gift – perhaps as a house-warming present, or for someone who loves cooking.

1 Prepare the pot by cutting the cinnamon sticks to the length of the pot and gluing them in position. Trim the top of the larger cone. Cut the smaller cone to fit inside the pot.

2 Put four stub (floral) wires upright in the pot so they project above the foam. Use these wires to stake the trimmed cone on top of the foam-filled pot.

3 Sort out all the complete star anise from the pack, plus any that are almost complete – you'll need about 20 in all. Wire these up by passing a wire over the front in one direction, and another wire over the front in another direction to make a cross of wires. Twist the wires together at the back and trim to about 1 cm (½ in).

4 Start by arranging the star anise in rows down the cone – about three each side to quarter the cone. Put two vertically between each line. Next, just fill the whole remaining area of cone with cloves, packing them tightly so none of the foam shows through.

5 Glue two short pieces of cinnamon stick into a cross. Wire this up, and use it to decorate the top of the topiary.

VALENTINE DECORATION IN A BOX

This display, in a heart-shaped box, demonstrates that dried flowers and seedheads look very striking and attractive when massed in groups of one type. Filled with romantic roses and scented lavender, this display can be made as a gift for Valentine's Day or simply as a treat for yourself. It can also be made at any other time of year using a different shaped box.

MATERIALS

1 block plastic foam for dried flowers
knife
heart-shaped box
scissors
1 bunch red roses
2 bunches lavender
2 bunches poppy seedheads
1 bunch Nigella orientalis

1 Stand the block of plastic foam on its end and carefully slice in half down its length with a knife. Then shape both pieces, using the box as a template, so that they will each fit into one half of the box. Fit these two halves into the heart-shaped box, ensuring that they fit snugly.

2 Divide the heart shape into quarters, separating each section by a line of the materials to be used. Fill one quarter with rose heads, one with lavender, one with poppy seedheads and the last with *Nigella orientalis*. Make sure that all the material heads are at the same level.

TIP

This arrangement is easy to make, but for the best effect do not scrimp on materials. The flower heads need to be massed together very tightly to hide the foam.

VALENTINE POT POURRI

This is a wonderful way of making use of spare flower pieces from other displays. This is not so long-lasting as pot pourri made the traditional way, but it's a quick and effective method when time is short.

MATERIALS

box
red and pink rosebuds, or any suitable assortment
lavender
scissors
reindeer moss
rose or lavender essential oil

TIP

The plain cardboard box used for this mixture has been covered with a broad red ribbon, and a piece of the same ribbon has been cut in half to create the decoration on the top of the box. Essential oil will discolour the materials in the box over a period of time. To avoid this, let the essential oil drops fall only on to the moss; with the lid closed the gentle perfume will still be imparted to the flowers.

1 Line the bottom of the box with rosebuds and a few stems of lavender. Trim the stems of the lavender fairly short, using mostly the flower heads.

2 Place some of the reindeer moss in the box, around the rosebuds and flower heads.

3 Trim the heads from the stems of all the remaining flowers and arrange them in the box. Add a few fresh flower heads if you wish, but make sure they are not too woody, otherwise they won't dry out.

4 Gently drizzle a few drops of the essential oil over the reindeer moss, to give the flowers a pleasantly gentle perfume.

HORSESHOE BABY GIFT

What could be nicer for new parents than to receive a floral symbol of good luck on the birth of their baby? The whites and pale green of this horseshoe make it a perfect gift or decoration for the nursery.

MATERIALS

14 stems white roses
42 stems bleached honesty
60 stems natural phalaris
scissors
silver wire
florist's (stem-wrap) tape
stub (floral) wires
ribbon

1 Cut the rose stems, honesty stems and phalaris to approximately 2.5 cm (1 in) long. Double leg mount the roses individually on silver wire, then tape. Double leg mount the phalaris heads in groups of five on silver wire, and the honesty in clusters of three also on silver wire. Tape each individual group.

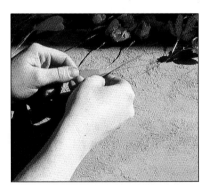

2 Make a stay wire approximately 30 cm (12 in) long from stub (floral) wire on which the horseshoe will be built.

3 Form three small bows about 4 cm (1½ in) wide from the ribbon and bind them at their centres with silver wire. Cut a 30 cm (12 in) length of ribbon and double leg mount both ends separately with silver wire. This will form the handle for the horseshoe.

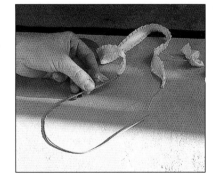

4 Make a horseshoe shape with the stay wire. Tape one wired end of the ribbon to one end of the stay wire. Tape one of the bows over the junction of the ribbon and stay wire, making sure it is securely in place.

5 Starting at the bow, tape the flowers and foliage to the stay wire, to its mid point, following this repeating sequence: phalaris, rose, honesty. Tape a bow at the centre and tape the last bow and the last ribbon end to the other end of the stay wire. Work the flowers using the same sequence back to the centre point of the horseshoe.

BRIDESMAID'S POMANDER

Popular in Victorian England, traditional, sweet-smelling pomanders make an interesting adornment for bridesmaids. This uncomplicated version is built around a plastic foam ball, using head-to-head roses interspersed with eucalyptus.

MATERIALS

stub (floral) wire
1 plastic foam ball for dried flowers
red ribbon
scissors
red roses
glue gun
glycerined eucalyptus

1 Bend a long stub (floral) wire in half and push the wire ends into the foam until both ends protrude, and there is only a little metal loop left at the other end. Now bend the wire ends back and pull them back into the ball.

2 Attach a length of ribbon securely to the loop end. Remove all the rose heads from their stems.

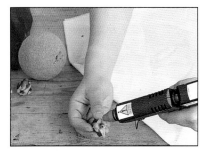

3 Using a glue gun, place a drop of glue on the underside of the rose heads and stick the heads to the plastic foam ball.

4 Begin by making a circle of roses all around the middle, working from top to bottom.

5 Now turn the pomander 90 degrees and stick another row of roses down the centre, dividing the pomander into quarters.

6 Fill in the quarters with the remaining rose heads, and then begin to insert small pieces of eucalyptus between the rose heads to hide any holes.

7 Take the two ends of the ribbon and tie a knot to the required length. If a small child is to carry the pomander, do not make the handle too long. Finish with a bow.

SUMMER WEDDING PEW END

*A collection of these set high on the ends of the church pews produces
a dramatic effect, especially if all the candles are burning. These pew ends
can be made without the candle, and in a range of different sizes.
Keep the stems fairly long to give a balanced shape to the finished piece.*

MATERIALS

*2 canes 60 cm (24 in) long
40-45 cm (16-18 in) candle
florist's adhesive tape
pink larkspur
pink roses
stub (floral) wires
raffia
scissors*

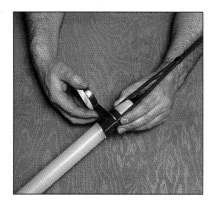

1 Place a cane on either side of the base of the candle. Hold them in place with florist's adhesive tape. Make sure the canes are firmly taped in place as tightly as possible.

2 Arrange a layer of flowers around the candle, with the heads just above the height of the tape fixing, holding them in place. Add more material to create a large posy with the candle in the middle.

TIP
When making a large display from a fairly small amount of material, the trick is constantly to criss-cross the stems as the display is built up.

3 Criss-cross the stems, at an outward angle, to produce a wide, circular display. Tie a stub (floral) wire around the stems and fix it firmly. Tie a raffia bow around the middle to cover the wire and attach a strong S-shaped wire at the back to attach the pew end to the fixing on the church pew.

BRIDAL BOUQUET

The romance of roses, the veil-like quality of gypsophila and the luxury of Singapore orchids are gathered together in this bouquet that could be carried by the bride or her attendants, and then kept as a memento of the happy day.

MATERIALS

scissors
pastel-mauve dyed sea lavender
stub (floral) wires
florist's silver roll wire
wire cutters
white florist's (stem wrap) tape
hydrangea
gypsophila
Singapore orchids
cream roses
purple statice
lady's mantle
strawflowers
pampas leaves
broom sprays
4 cm (1½ in) wide satin ribbon in two toning colours

TIP

To avoid crushing the delicate flowers, place the bouquet in a deep vase or other container until the wedding day. To preserve the bouquet, keep it well away from strong light.

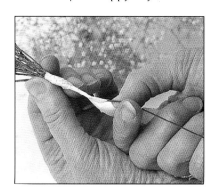

1 Cut short sprays of sea lavender. Place a stub (floral) wire close against the stems and bind with silver roll wire. Bind the stems and false wire stem with florist's (stem wrap) tape. Bind clusters of hydrangea bracts, gypsophila and short-stemmed roses in a similar way.

2 Gather together several flower sprays and foliage stems and arrange them in one hand so that they cascade in a natural, easy way. Rearrange until the combination is pleasing, then bind the group of false stems together with silver roll wire.

3 Add more wired and bound stems to the group, a few at a time. Alternate the full, round shapes of roses and strawflowers with wispy sprays of gypsophila and lady's mantle. Bind the bunch of false stems with ribbon, overlapping each twist all the way down. To finish, tie more ribbons around the handle to create large bows with long, trailing ends.

ROSE PARCEL

To make a present extra special why not make the wrapping a part of the gift?
This display could not be simpler, but the finished effect is very pretty.

MATERIALS

boxed present
tissue paper
pressed flowers
handmade paper with petals
garden twine
sealing wax
3 stems roses
gift tag

1 Cover the box with several layers of tissue paper. Scatter pressed flowers on the top before wrapping around the handmade paper.

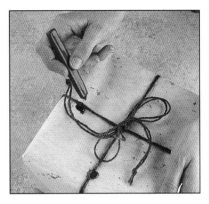

2 Tie a double length of garden twine around the parcel, then finish off with a bow. Drip sealing wax on to the string to secure it.

3 Tuck three dried roses under the twine, write a message on a gift tag and tie it on to the bow.

TIP
Very quick and easy to make, the simplicity of this charming gift-wrap decoration is irresistible.

CHRISTMAS CANDLE POT DISPLAY

This display is designed to make the most of the rich, dark colours
of Christmas and to hint at the large variety of edible treats
we expect at this special time of the year.

MATERIALS

knife
1 block plastic foam for dried flowers
terracotta flowerpot
glue gun
stub (floral) wires
candle
hay
red amaranthus
cones
magnolia leaves
holly oak
kutchi fruit
twigs
chillies
oranges
cinnamon sticks
lavender
mushrooms
fresh moss
raffia
cutters

TIP

To create a richer look, spray the display with a clear florist's lacquer and lightly frost it with gold paint. Attach a gold fabric bow to the pot with a glue gun and replace the plain church candle with a candle that is heavily perfumed with spices.

1 Trim the foam block to fit snugly into the terracotta pot. Glue or wire the candle to the foam block. Fit the block into the pot. Wire the materials and start to push them into the foam base. Balance is very important: add the ingredients on alternate sides of the display, starting with the larger items. At this stage, the display ingredients will seem to have a lot of space between them, but as the items are added the whole design will begin to take shape.

2 Add all the smaller items – the chillies, oranges, cinnamon sticks, lavender, and so on – filling the spaces between the larger items. Trim with the moss, using a glue gun or U-shaped stub (floral) wires, so that no foam base shows. The moss can also be used to fill any large gaps between the materials, but be careful not to use too much moss or the general look will be lost. Take particular care to moss around the candle base to cover the fixings.

EVERLASTING CHRISTMAS TREE

*This delightful little tree, made from dyed, preserved oak leaves
and decorated with tiny gilded cones, would make an enchanting
Christmas decoration.*

MATERIALS

knife
1 bunch of dyed, dried oak leaves
florist's silver roll wire
small fir cones
picture framer's wax gilt
terracotta pot, 18 cm (7 in) tall
*1 small plastic foam cone for
dried flowers*
4 stub (floral) wires
*1 plastic foam cone for dried flowers,
18 cm (7 in) tall*

1 Cut the leaves off the branches
and trim the stalks. Wire up
bunches of about four leaves, making
some bunches with small leaves,
some with medium-size leaves and
others with large leaves. Sort the
bunches into piles.

2 Insert wires into the bottom end
of each fir cone and twist the
ends together. Gild each cone by
rubbing on wax gilt.

TIP
You could make several small
arrangements and then group them
together to make a wonderfully
festive centrepiece, or place one at
each place setting.

3 Prepare the pot by cutting the
smaller foam cone to fit the pot,
adding stub (floral) wire stakes and
positioning the larger cone on to this.
Attach the leaf bunches to the cone,
starting at the top with the small
leaves, and working down through
the medium and large leaves to make
a realistic shape. Add the gilded
cones to finish.

Index